THE NERVOUS SYSTEM

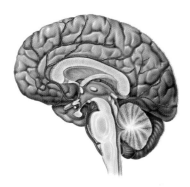

For a free color catalog describing Gareth Stevens' list of high-quality books and multimedia programs, call 1-800-542-2595 (USA) or 1-800-461-9120 (Canada). Gareth Stevens Publishing's Fax: (414) 225-0377. See our catalog, too, on the World Wide Web: gsinc.com

The editor would like to extend special thanks to Ronald J. Gerrits, Ph.D. (Physiology), Medical College of Wisconsin, Milwaukee, Wisconsin, for his kind and professional help with the information in this book.

Library of Congress Cataloging-in-Publication Data

Llamas, Andreu.
    [Sistema nerviosa. English]
    The nervous system / by Andreu Llamas ; illustrated by Luis Rizo.
      p. cm. — (The human body)
    Includes bibliographical references and index.
    Summary: Explains the structures and functions of the central nervous system (brain and spinal cord) and the peripheral nervous system including the autonomic systems.
    ISBN 0-8368-2113-0 (lib. bdg.)
    1. Neurophysiology—Juvenile literature. 2. Nervous system—Juvenile literature.
[1. Nervous system.] I. Rizo, Luis, ill. II. Title. III. Series: Llamas, Andreu.
The human body.
QP361.5.L5313 1998
612.8—dc21   98-6645

First published in North America in 1998 by
Gareth Stevens Publishing
1555 North RiverCenter Drive, Suite 201
Milwaukee, WI 53212 USA

This U.S. edition © 1998 by Gareth Stevens, Inc.
Original edition © 1996 by Ediciones Lema, S. L., Barcelona, Spain.
Additional end matter © 1998 by Gareth Stevens, Inc.

U.S. series editor: Rita Reitci
Editorial assistant: Diane Laska

Printed in Mexico

1 2 3 4 5 6 7 8 9 02 01 00 99 98

Gareth Stevens Publishing
MILWAUKEE

The Nervous System

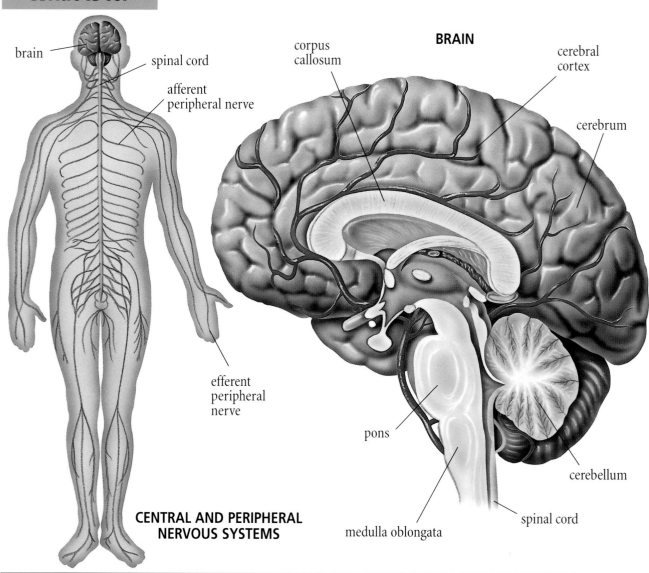

brain

spinal cord

afferent peripheral nerve

efferent peripheral nerve

CENTRAL AND PERIPHERAL NERVOUS SYSTEMS

BRAIN

corpus callosum

cerebral cortex

cerebrum

pons

cerebellum

medulla oblongata

spinal cord

A living computer. Did you know that the human body's nervous system is more complicated than the most advanced computer in the world?

The human nervous system coordinates all the activities and functions of the body — 24 hours a day, every day. This system is usually divided into central and peripheral structures.

The central nervous system consists of the brain and the spinal cord, connecting through the medulla oblongata. The brain contains the control center, which receives information from all parts of the body and sends out orders through the spinal cord.

The peripheral nervous system is an extensive and complex network of nerves that connects the central nervous system with the different organs of the body; for example, the sense organs. The peripheral nervous system sends information to the central nervous system through the afferent sensory nerves. It then transmits any instructions along the efferent motor nerves. The peripheral system is divided into the somatic nervous system, which controls the movements of the skeletal muscles, and the autonomic nervous system, which automatically controls the function of such important organs as the heart, stomach, and others.

BRAIN
(Cross section)

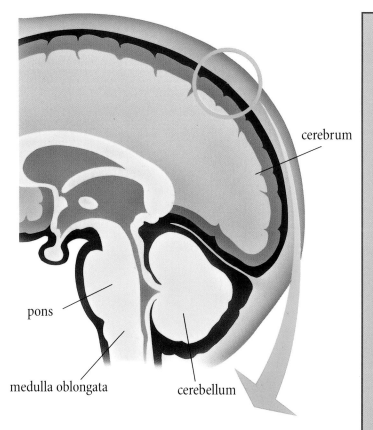

cerebrum

pons

medulla oblongata

cerebellum

Protecting the brain. The largest part of the skull, the cranium, protects the brain. The most important parts of the brain are: cerebrum, cerebellum, pons, and medulla oblongata. The cerebrum, the largest, occupies most of the cranium. The smaller cerebellum, located behind the cerebrum, keeps humans balanced and controls movements.

The brain is so vital that it has several means of protection. First, it is covered by the hard bony cranium. Beneath the cranium is a series of membranes called meninges. Meninges form padding to save the brain from friction and any strikes against the skull's interior. The three meninges are: the dura mater, the outermost and strongest, which separates into two layers in some areas, creating a venous sinus through which blood flows; the arachnoid; and the pia mater, the innermost and thinnest membrane. An infection in the meninges causes meningitis, an illness that can be fatal.

The space between the pia mater and the arachnoid is filled with cerebrospinal fluid, which acts as a shock absorber for the brain. Without this protection, a blow to the head would injure the brain.

Another function of the cerebrospinal fluid is to supply the cerebrum and the medulla oblongata with nutrients.

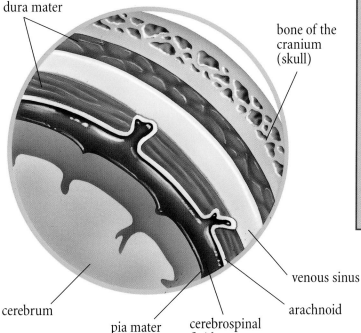

dura mater

bone of the cranium (skull)

venous sinus

arachnoid

cerebrum

pia mater

cerebrospinal fluid

STRUCTURES THAT PROTECT THE BRAIN
(Enlarged view)

The Neurons

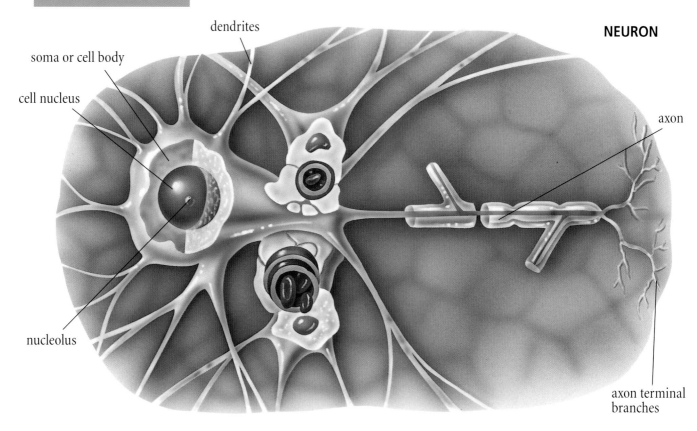

soma or cell body

cell nucleus

dendrites

NEURON

axon

nucleolus

axon terminal branches

Nerve pathways. Nervous tissue is formed by nerve cells, or neurons. Each neuron has a soma, or central cell body, with a nucleus inside it, and some dendrites that communicate with other neurons to form the nervous pathways.

The bodies of the neurons have different sizes and shapes, depending on the job they do in the organ where they are located.

All neurons have one or more dendrites in the form of treelike branches. Each also has a single longer and thicker "trunk," called the axon. The axon communicates with the cells, forming the nervous pathways of communication. In this way, neurons can actually contact thousands of other neurons.

The cerebral cortex, or outer layer of the brain, is formed only from the bodies of the neurons, resulting in gray matter. The white matter making up most of the interior of the cerebrum is formed

from the axons of the neurons. In the spinal cord, just the opposite situation occurs. The outer part is formed from the white matter. The interior is composed of gray matter.

Axons can be very long. In humans, the axons that run down the legs from the base of the spine measure about 3 feet (1 meter). Each axon can split into more than 10,000 terminals, or branches, with each branch connecting with another neuron. Because each neuron can receive messages from more than a thousand other neurons, a single neuron can have more than a million different conversations simultaneously!

All neurons are different from the rest of the cells in one important way. They are unable to multiply. When neurons die, they are not replaced by new ones. This means the human body has more neurons in youth than at an older age.

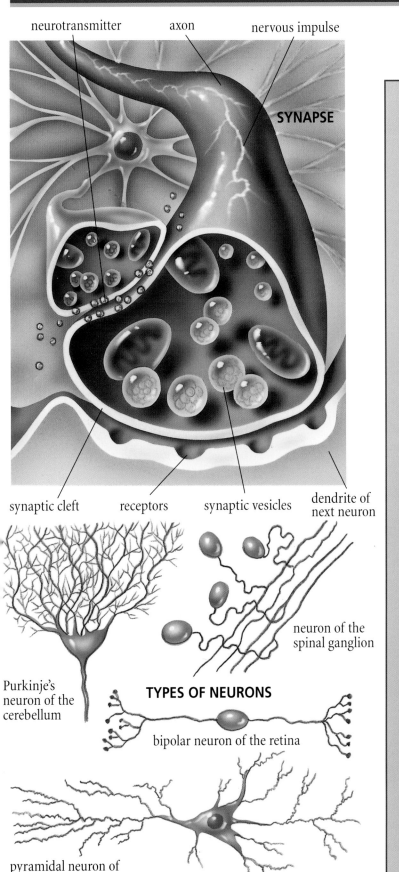

neurotransmitter   axon   nervous impulse

SYNAPSE

synaptic cleft   receptors   synaptic vesicles   dendrite of next neuron

Purkinje's neuron of the cerebellum

neuron of the spinal ganglion

TYPES OF NEURONS

bipolar neuron of the retina

pyramidal neuron of the cerebral cortex

Transmitting nerve impulses. Each neuron has various short, tiny branches called dendrites and a single long stalk called an axon. When axons leave the spinal cord, they group together in bundles, or nerves. These nerves carry the nervous impulses, which are electro-chemical in nature, to other neurons.

Most neurons do not touch one another. A gap, called the synaptic cleft, lies between the axon's terminal and the neighboring neuron's dendrites. Contact, or synapse, takes place across this gap. There, the nervous impulses go from one neuron to the next one. The impulse always travels in the same direction, from the axon of one neuron to the dendrite of the next one. This gap is so tiny that nervous impulses can travel very quickly from one neuron to the neighboring one.

When the electrical impulse reaches the axon's terminal, it causes the release of neurotransmitters. These are chemical substances that carry messages from one side of the synaptic cleft to the other. There, they fit receptors on the dendrites of the neighboring neuron. This process takes place at great speed.

The neurotransmitters stimulate the neighboring neuron. In some instances, the neurotransmitters prevent, or inhibit, the receiving neuron from producing an electric impulse.

Sensory neurons, or afferents, do the job of receiving the stimuli from the outer world. Most of them are located in the sense organs. Motor neurons, or efferents, transmit nervous impulses to muscles, glands, and organs.

The Nerves

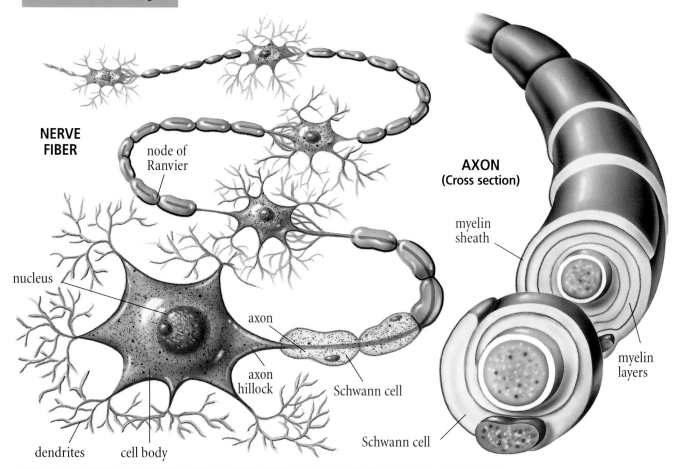

NERVE FIBER

node of Ranvier

AXON
(Cross section)

myelin sheath

nucleus

axon

axon hillock

Schwann cell

dendrites   cell body

Schwann cell

myelin layers

Chains of neurons. A nerve fiber is formed by a chain of nerve cells, or neurons. Nerve fibers are extensions of the nerve cells that leave the spine through the intervertebral foramina. These are openings between the vertebrae of the vertebral column. The nerves are bundles, or groups, of very thin nerve fibers that arise from the spinal cord.

All sensations, such as pain, cold, heat, taste, and smell, in addition to the orders sent to different parts of the body, come and go from the brain and the spinal cord through a complex network of nerves.

The somatic nervous system connects the central nervous system with the sense organs and with the skeletal, or voluntary, muscles. This system has two kinds of nerves, cranial and spinal.

Cranial nerves consist of 12 pairs of nerves leading to the head, neck, and the main organs in the body.

Spinal nerves consist of 31 pairs of nerves coming out of the spinal cord and going to different parts of the body.

Nerve fibers are made up mostly of axons. The axon, which transmits the nerve impulse, is covered with a sheath made from a fatty substance called myelin. The myelin sheath forms during embryonic development when Schwann cells wrap around the axon. Some nerve fibers have a thinner myelin sheath than others. The myelin sheath insulates the axon, allowing nerve impulses to be transmitted faster. In myelinated axons, nerve impulses can travel at speeds of about 290 miles (465 kilometers) per hour!

Some axons inside the brain and in the spinal cord do not have myelin sheaths. Because of this, nerve impulses in these axons travel slower.

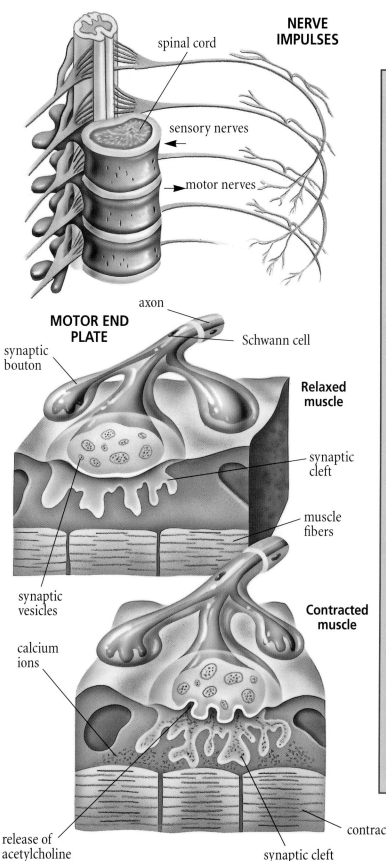

NERVE IMPULSES

spinal cord

sensory nerves

motor nerves

MOTOR END PLATE

axon

Schwann cell

synaptic bouton

Relaxed muscle

synaptic cleft

muscle fibers

synaptic vesicles

Contracted muscle

calcium ions

release of acetylcholine

synaptic cleft

contracted fibers

Orders from the brain go to the spinal cord. From there, they travel to all parts of the body through the nerves.

Types of nerves. Some groups of nerves go to the voluntary, or skeletal, muscles; others reach the sense organs; and still others contact other organs of the body. In each case, the nerves have different functions. In the peripheral nervous system, information always travels in the same direction. The dendrites of sensory nerves are located in the sense organs and in the skin. These nerves send sensations and stimuli from the different parts of the body to the spinal cord and the brain, where they are interpreted. Motor nerves then send the orders from the nerve centers to the different areas in the body along the axon, and these terminate in the muscle fibers. Some nerves have only afferent (sensory) fibers; others have only efferent (motor) fibers; while mixed nerves have both kinds of fibers.

The motor plates. Motor nerves end in what are known as motor end plates on muscle fibers. The terminal axon has tiny branches, each ending in a swelling called a synaptic bouton; together these form the motor end plate. This plate is separated from the muscle fiber by a synaptic cleft.

Vesicles inside each synaptic bouton contain acetylcholine, a neurotransmitter. A nerve impulse releases acetylcholine, which then causes calcium ions to contract muscle fibers.

The Cerebrum

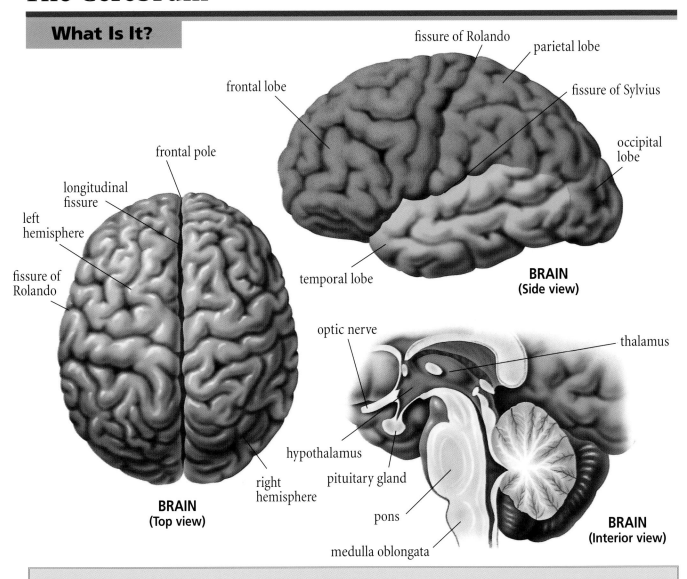

fissure of Rolando

parietal lobe

frontal lobe

fissure of Sylvius

occipital lobe

frontal pole

longitudinal fissure

left hemisphere

fissure of Rolando

temporal lobe

BRAIN
(Side view)

optic nerve

thalamus

hypothalamus

right hemisphere

pituitary gland

pons

BRAIN
(Top view)

medulla oblongata

BRAIN
(Interior view)

Divisions. The cerebrum is the biggest structure of the brain. It weighs about 3 pounds (1.4 kilograms) in men and about 2.75 pounds (1.25 kg) in women. It is made up of 50,000 to 100,000 million neurons.

Fissures, or grooves, divide the cerebrum's folded surface. The longitudinal fissure divides the cerebrum into two symmetrical halves, or hemispheres: right and left. Each hemisphere is divided crosswise by two fissures: the fissure of Rolando and the fissure of Sylvius.

The cerebrum is divided into four lobes, each taking its name from the bone that protects it. These are, from front to back: frontal, temporal, parietal, and occipital. Cavities, filled with cerebrospinal fluid, connect the four lobes.

The cerebral cortex is a thin layer covering the cerebrum. It is gray matter, formed by bodies of neurons, or nerve cells.

White matter makes up the rest of the cerebral tissue. This is composed of the axons of the nerve cells. Under the cortex lie the most primitive structures of the brain. These do the work of controlling a great number of basic functions in the body.

The corpus callosum is formed by a bundle of many axons. It is located beneath the longitudinal fissure, and connects the two hemispheres so that the body will work as a unit. The speech center in most people is located in the left hemisphere. The corpus callosum also forms a communication network between the cerebellum and the cerebral cortex.

THALAMUS AND HYPOTHALAMUS
(Cross section)

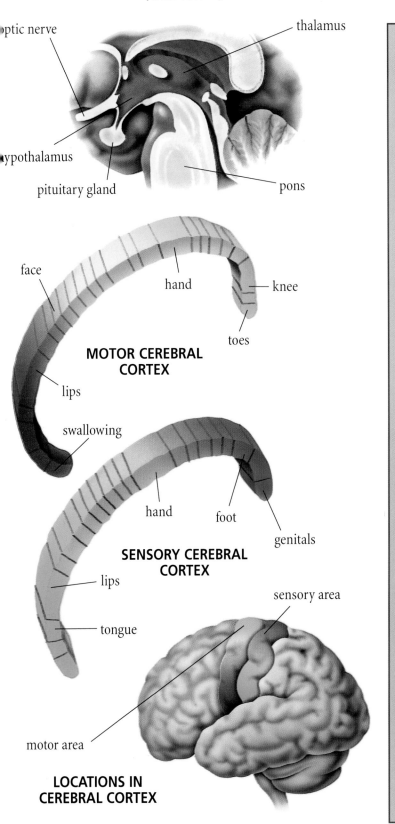

optic nerve

thalamus

hypothalamus

pituitary gland

pons

face

hand

knee

toes

**MOTOR CEREBRAL
CORTEX**

lips

swallowing

hand

foot

genitals

**SENSORY CEREBRAL
CORTEX**

lips

tongue

sensory area

motor area

**LOCATIONS IN
CEREBRAL CORTEX**

Most of the body's areas of control are located in the brain's cerebral cortex. *(Illustrations are not in proportion.)*

The thalamus. This area inside the brain is made up of gray matter. Nerve impulses received by each of the sense organs go first to the thalamus. This analyzes and correlates the impulses received and then sends these on to the sensory area of the cerebral cortex, where they are felt as conscious sensations.

The hypothalamus. This area of the brain, located below the thalamus, acts as a bridge between the nervous and the endocrine systems. It controls and regulates the autonomic system and the metabolic state of the body. It is formed by groups of cells called hypothalamic nuclei, each of which controls such functions as the body's temperature, appetite, thirst, and sleep.

The hypothalamus is connected to other areas of the nervous system. It serves as a receiver and transmitter of messages, carrying impulses to and from the cerebral cortex, the sense organs, the digestive system, and other areas of the body. The hypothalamus also regulates some functions of the pituitary, which is a gland that secretes hormones. One of these hormones, somatotropin, controls the body's growth.

The hypothalamus is an all-around regulator of body functions. It maintains internal temperature and fluid balance. In addition, the hypothalamus controls the sensations of hunger and thirst. It also releases hormones that take part in growth and sexual activity.

The Nerve Centers of the Cerebrum

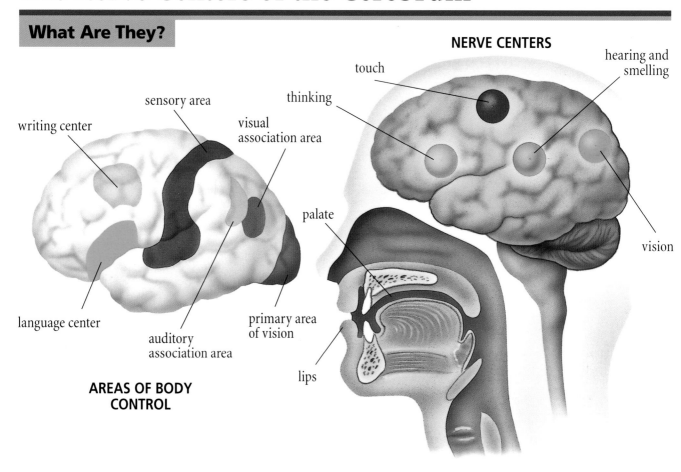

NERVE CENTERS

touch

hearing and smelling

thinking

sensory area

visual association area

writing center

palate

vision

language center

primary area of vision

auditory association area

lips

AREAS OF BODY CONTROL

Control centers. The information received by the brain from the sense organs is interpreted in different sensory areas, or nerve centers.

Many impulses travel along nerve pathways to gray matter, formed by billions of neurons. From there, the brain controls the functions of the body, ordering and coordinating the movements of voluntary muscles.

The thickness of the cortex ranges from 0.06-.18 inch (1.5-4.5 millimeters), according to the area. Nerve centers that interpret, register, and store messages from the senses are in this thin layer.

These centers also control and regulate the body's movements and such important functions as intelligence, will, and memory.

Scientists have discovered that, while some nerve centers are distributed over all the cortex, others are located in distinct centers. In the frontal lobe lies the center that creates thoughts. The center of touch is located in the parietal lobe. The temporal lobe contains the centers of hearing and smell. A center of vision is located within each occipital lobe.

Next to each of these centers lies a memory center for that sense. For example, the visual memory center can be compared to a file of photographs of all the objects a person knows. By comparing what the person sees with visual memories, the person can identify objects as soon as they are presented.

The stimuli coming from the voluntary muscular system — the muscles under conscious control — go to a voluntary muscle sensory area, located in the parietal lobe.

Orders to move one or more muscles go out from the motor area, which is in the frontal lobe. These two areas control a great number of muscles, from the tips of the toes to the muscles in the head. This is a very complex job!

ORGANS CONTROLLED BY CRANIAL NERVES

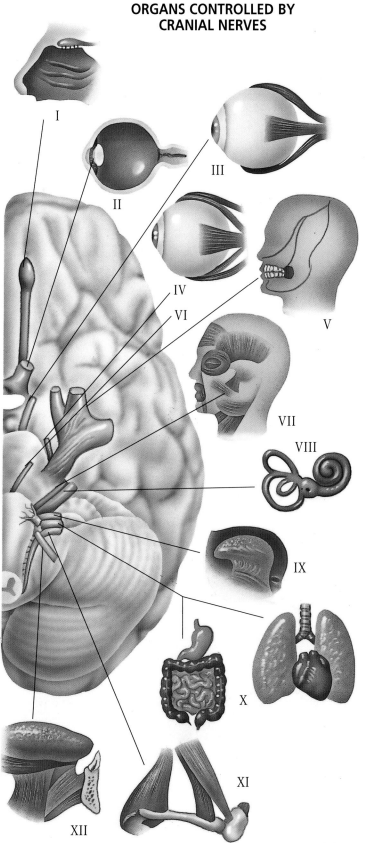

Cranial nerves. Cranial nerves occur in pairs. They are labeled with Roman numerals — *see illustration at left.*

I. Olfactory nerve: sends olfactory sensations, or odors, from the upper nasal cavities to the brain.

II. Optic nerve: sends visual impulses from the retina to the cerebrum.

III. Oculomotor nerve: controls some movements of eyeball; constricts pupil.

IV. Trochlear nerve: controls movements of the optic muscles.

V. Trigeminal nerve: sends sensations to the brain from face, scalp, and teeth; contracts chewing muscles.

VI. Aducens nerve: controls lateral, or sideways, movement of the eyeball.

VII. Facial nerve: causes movement of various facial muscles; sends tastes from tongue to the cerebrum; secretes saliva.

VIII. Auditory nerve: sends auditory and balance signals from inner ear to brain.

IX. Glosspharyngeal nerve: controls swallowing muscles of pharynx; sends taste sensations from back of tongue; secretes saliva; sensory for heart, breathing, blood pressure reflexes.

X. Vagus nerve: controls the larynx, esophagus, heart, lungs, some abdominal organs; increases digestive secretions.

XI. Spinal accessory nerve: controls the movement of some neck muscles and the muscles of larynx in speaking.

XII. Hypoglossal nerve: controls movement of the tongue muscles in speaking, chewing, and swallowing.

The Cerebellum and Medulla Oblongata

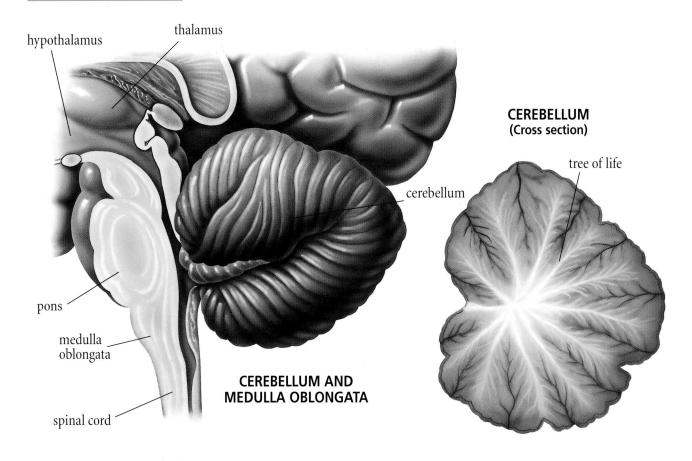

hypothalamus

thalamus

CEREBELLUM
(Cross section)

tree of life

cerebellum

pons

medulla
oblongata

CEREBELLUM AND
MEDULLA OBLONGATA

spinal cord

Relay stations. The cerebellum is one-eighth the size of the cerebrum. It is located at the back of the skull, just below the occipital lobes of the cerebrum. It has two layers: an outer layer, or cerebral cortex, of gray matter, and an inner layer of white matter.

The cortex, or outer layer, is formed by three layers of gray matter. The most important layer is the middle, formed by Purkinje cells. These are very long and complex nerve cells. Each interconnects with more than 100,000 cells!

The cerebellum is divided into right and left hemispheres. Its cortex is highly folded. In fact, 85 percent of the surface is covered by these innumerable folds. A cross section of the cerebellum shows white nerve fibers split into many branches, resembling the branches of a tree. This structure is often called the tree of life.

The cerebellum develops very quickly after birth. A two-year-old child's cerebellum is almost as big as the cerebellum of an adult.

The pons is a meeting point of many nerve pathways. It lies below the occipital lobes. The pons acts as a relay station, transmitting sensations from the body's sensory pathways to the brain. It also carries nerve impulses from the cerebrum and cerebellum to the motor pathways of the spinal cord. The pons has two respiratory centers that work with those in the medulla oblongata to produce normal breathing.

The medulla oblongata is an extension of the pons and is directly connected to the spinal cord. It carries all the nerve pathways from the brain to the spinal cord. It also helps regulate the body's involuntary functions, such as breathing and the beating of the heart.

NERVE CENTERS COORDINATING MOVEMENT

suppression area

motor area

thalamus

nerve pathway

cerebellum

spinal cord

CEREBELLUM
(Enlarged view)

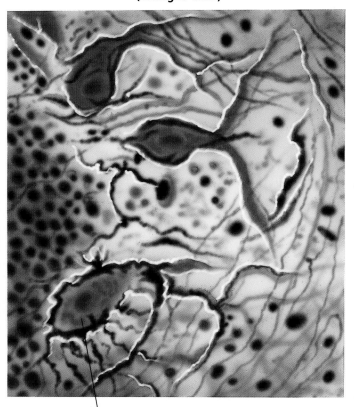

Purkinje cells

The work of the cerebellum. The cerebellum automatically coordinates the functions of the other parts of the brain so that orders will be followed correctly and without interruption.

Knowing how to move. The cerebellum coordinates the movements of the locomotor system originating in the cerebrum and also controls equilibrium, or balance.

It does this by knowing how the body's weight is distributed between various areas in the body, and how the head, neck, and remainder of the body are positioned. The cerebellum is vital to the control of all movements of the body, such as the ability to walk, run, and jump.

Learning new patterns. When learning a sequence of actions, the cerebellum needs constant supervision by the cerebrum. However, when the cerebellum has learned the correct sequence, it can control and carry out the actions by itself. The cerebellum stores learned sequences, which are activated by the cerebral cortex.

The movements start in the motor cortex, but they are instantly changed (modified) by the adjacent cortical suppression area before they are transmitted to the muscles. The cerebellum and the thalamus examine and correct every muscular movement. The cerebellum unconsciously coordinates these movements.

Data storage. The information reaching the cerebellum is registered in large special neurons called Purkinje cells. These cells constantly update the picture of the body's position in relation to the outer world. Each Purkinje cell can receive information from more than 100,000 different neurons.

The Autonomic Nervous System

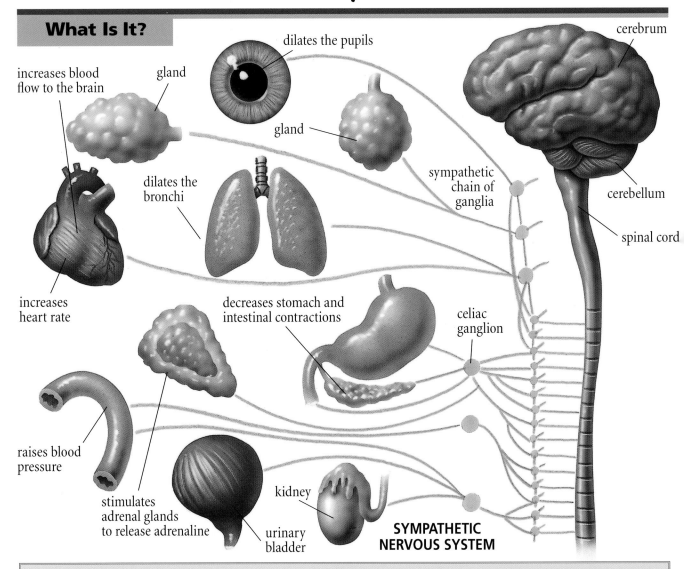

increases blood flow to the brain

gland

dilates the pupils

gland

cerebrum

sympathetic chain of ganglia

cerebellum

spinal cord

dilates the bronchi

increases heart rate

decreases stomach and intestinal contractions

celiac ganglion

raises blood pressure

stimulates adrenal glands to release adrenaline

urinary bladder

kidney

SYMPATHETIC NERVOUS SYSTEM

Controlling internal organs. The autonomic nervous system regulates the functions of the organs in the body. This allows functions to adjust to each specific circumstance humans meet. The autonomic nervous system has two different divisions: the sympathetic nervous system, which stimulates the body and increases the expenditure of energy; and the parasympathetic system, which keeps the body calm and helps save energy.

The autonomic nervous system begins in a series of ganglia. Each ganglion is formed by a group of neurons outside the spinal cord. The preganglionic neurons from the sympathetic system (those preceding the ganglia) lie in the gray matter of the spinal cord, in the thoracic area and upper lumbar area. From there, nerve fibers run to the ganglia of the sympathetic chains, which lie on both sides of the vertebral column. These chains look like knotted ropes. From the ganglia, postganglionic nerve fibers go to the different organs that they control.

The fibers of the parasympathetic system come from the brain, medulla oblongata, and the sacral region of the spinal cord. Parasympathetic nerve fibers are found in cranial nerves III, VII, IX, and X.

The autonomic nervous system continuously sends impulses to the visceral, or internal, organs. The activity of these organs depends on the constant impulses sent to them by the sympathetic and parasympathetic systems. Most organs in the body receive fibers from the autonomic nervous system.

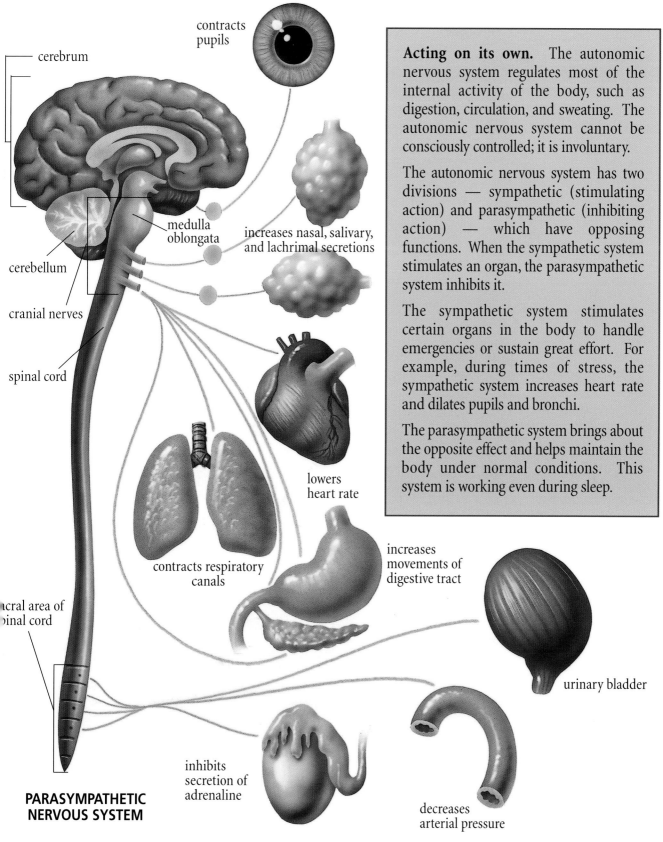

contracts pupils

cerebrum

medulla oblongata

increases nasal, salivary, and lachrimal secretions

cerebellum

cranial nerves

spinal cord

lowers heart rate

contracts respiratory canals

increases movements of digestive tract

ıcral area of ɔinal cord

urinary bladder

inhibits secretion of adrenaline

PARASYMPATHETIC NERVOUS SYSTEM

decreases arterial pressure

Acting on its own. The autonomic nervous system regulates most of the internal activity of the body, such as digestion, circulation, and sweating. The autonomic nervous system cannot be consciously controlled; it is involuntary.

The autonomic nervous system has two divisions — sympathetic (stimulating action) and parasympathetic (inhibiting action) — which have opposing functions. When the sympathetic system stimulates an organ, the parasympathetic system inhibits it.

The sympathetic system stimulates certain organs in the body to handle emergencies or sustain great effort. For example, during times of stress, the sympathetic system increases heart rate and dilates pupils and bronchi.

The parasympathetic system brings about the opposite effect and helps maintain the body under normal conditions. This system is working even during sleep.

The Spinal Cord

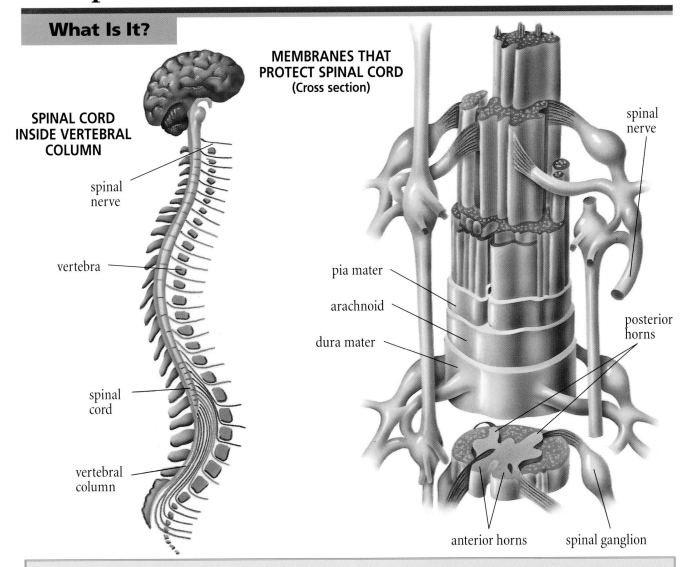

SPINAL CORD
INSIDE VERTEBRAL
COLUMN

spinal
nerve

vertebra

spinal
cord

vertebral
column

MEMBRANES THAT
PROTECT SPINAL CORD
(Cross section)

spinal
nerve

pia mater

arachnoid

dura mater

posterior
horns

anterior horns   spinal ganglion

The central nervous system. The brain and the spinal cord make up the central nervous system. The spinal cord is composed of neurons and nerve fibers. It begins at the occipital foramen in the skull, where it is directly joined to the medulla oblongata. Its lower end reaches the lumbar vertebrae. It measures 17 inches (42 centimeters) long and about 3/4 inch (2 cm) thick.

The spinal cord is protected by the vertebrae because it passes through the neural canal of the backbone. From there, the nerves of the peripheral nervous system travel to other areas of the body.

The spinal cord is also protected by the same meninges that protect the brain: dura mater, arachnoid, and pia mater. Cerebrospinal fluid between the pia mater and the arachnoid acts as a buffer and also provides nutrients to the spinal tissue. The protection is needed because spinal cord injuries can cause paralysis, or a loss of movement, in the body.

The spinal cord constitutes a communications network between the brain and the rest of the body. It carries considerable information in both directions. Sensory nerves carry stimuli from throughout the body to the cerebrum; motor nerves send orders from the brain to every part of the body. In cross section, the gray matter of the spinal cord looks like the letter H. The legs that are closer to the back are called posterior horns; those closer to the chest are known as anterior horns.

SPINAL REFLEX FROM A PAINFUL STIMULATION

sensory neuron

skin

painful stimulation

sensory impulse (afferent)

REACTION TO A PAINFUL STIMULATION

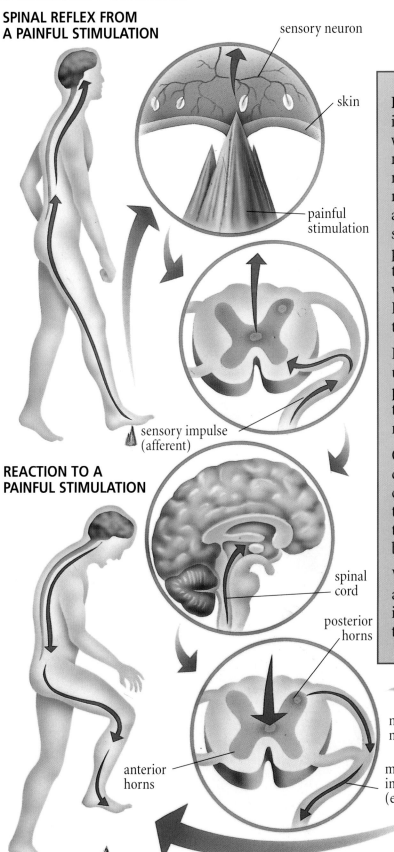

spinal cord

posterior horns

anterior horns

motor neuron

motor impulse (efferent)

muscle

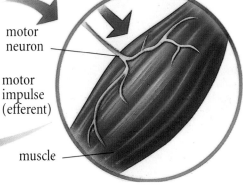

Reflexes. Most nervous system activity in humans is carried out automatically, without people having to think about it. A nerve impulse received by sensory receptors (of the skin or the senses) does not have to reach the cerebral cortex for action to take place. It just goes to the spinal cord, which sends a response. This process is known as a spinal reflex, and it takes place with the onset of injury. In this way, the body reacts quickly to danger. Besides the spinal cord reflex, signals go to the brain to be sensed as pain.

Inside the spinal cord, gray matter made up of millions of nerve cell bodies processes the sensory and motor messages that enter and leave. It also controls automatic reflexes.

Conscious activity depends on the orders coming from the motor areas of the cerebral cortex. Impulses go from there to the spinal cord, and from the spinal cord to the rest of the body. These actions involve both voluntary actions and reflexes.

When humans run, the autonomic system accelerates respiration and heart rate to increase the amount of blood that reaches the muscles.

The Peripheral Nervous System

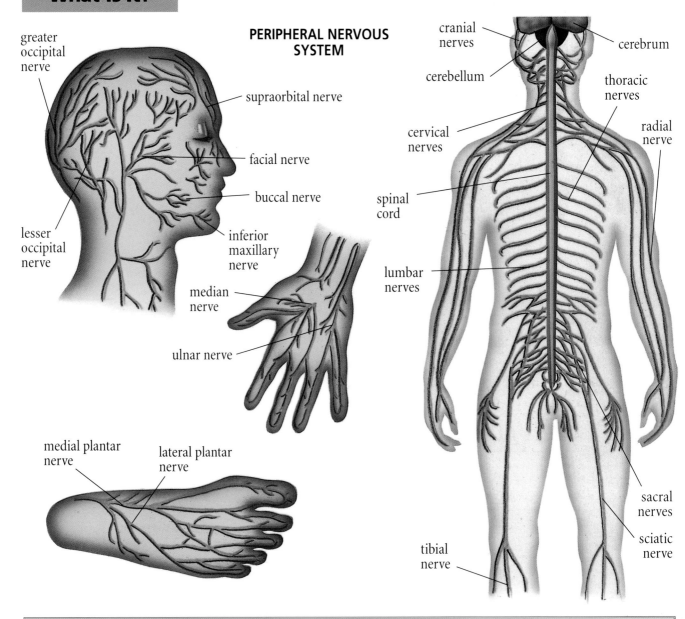

PERIPHERAL NERVOUS SYSTEM

greater occipital nerve

supraorbital nerve

facial nerve

buccal nerve

lesser occipital nerve

inferior maxillary nerve

median nerve

ulnar nerve

medial plantar nerve

lateral plantar nerve

cranial nerves

cerebrum

cerebellum

thoracic nerves

cervical nerves

radial nerve

spinal cord

lumbar nerves

sacral nerves

sciatic nerve

tibial nerve

A network of nerves. The peripheral nervous system, which includes the autonomic nervous system, goes from the brain and spinal cord to all parts of the human body.

Peripheral nerves carry messages in both directions, from the brain to the organs and muscles and back.

There are 31 pairs of spinal or somatic nerves, with hundreds of nerve cells. These leave the spinal cord through the intervertebral foramina, the openings between the vertebrae, and go around the body.

Some spinal nerves travel together during part of their journey, forming a network called a plexus.

Among the largest plexi are: the brachial plexus, in the area of the arms; the lumbar plexus, in the anterior thigh muscles and the skin of the legs; and the sacral plexus, in the posterior lower limbs.

The nerves forming the sacral plexus join to form the sciatic nerve. This major nerve can become inflamed, usually because of pressure on one of the nerve roots, producing painful sciatica.

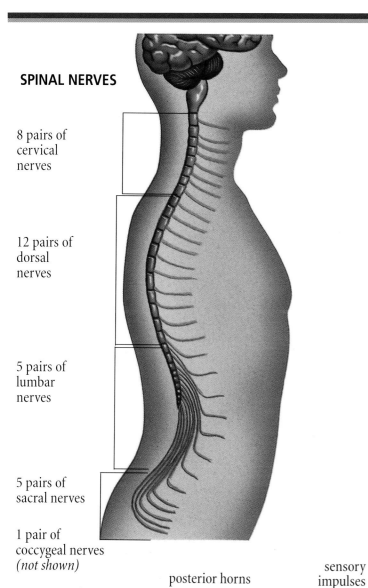

SPINAL NERVES

8 pairs of cervical nerves

12 pairs of dorsal nerves

5 pairs of lumbar nerves

5 pairs of sacral nerves

1 pair of coccygeal nerves *(not shown)*

Traveling impulses. Each spinal nerve has its origin in the gray matter of the spinal cord, where it forms two roots: the ventral and the dorsal. The anterior, or ventral, root comes from the anterior horns of the spinal cord. Motor impulses travel inside this root. The posterior, or dorsal, root comes from the posterior horns of the spinal cord; sensory stimuli travel through this root to the spinal cord.

After passing through intervertebral foramina, the two roots join together to form a spinal nerve. Each spinal nerve has an afferent nervous pathway transmitting sensory stimuli from the nerve endings to the spinal cord, and an efferent pathway sending motor impulses from the spinal cord to the organs and muscles.

Path of a nervous impulse. A stimulus travels from the place where it is detected (for example, the skin) to the sensory area of the brain, where it will be interpreted. This is a rapid process; an impulse generated by a stimulus in the skin can travel to the spinal cord at more than 426 feet (130 m) per second.

posterior horns

sensory impulses

white matter

SPINAL CORD (cross section)

gray matter

anterior horns

ventral root

dorsal root

motor impulses

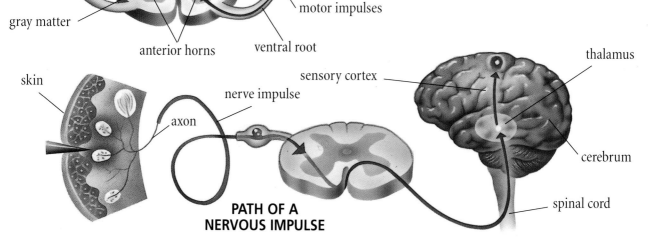

skin

nerve impulse

axon

sensory cortex

thalamus

cerebrum

spinal cord

PATH OF A NERVOUS IMPULSE

The Eye

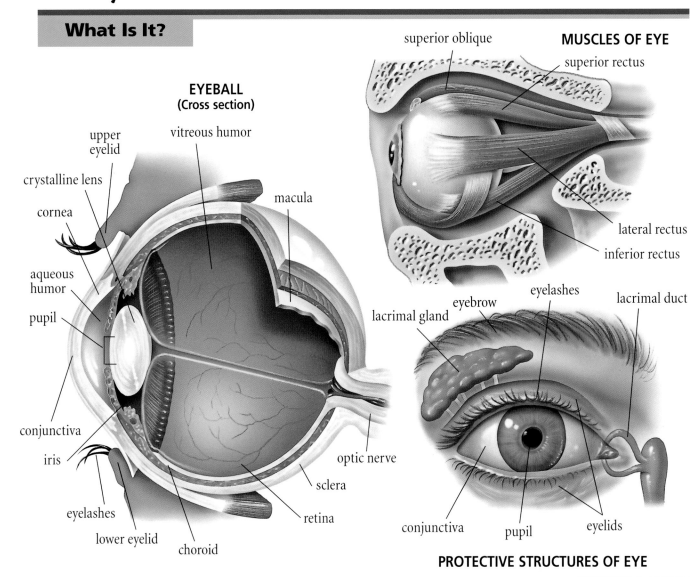

EYEBALL
(Cross section)

upper eyelid · vitreous humor · macula · crystalline lens · cornea · aqueous humor · pupil · conjunctiva · iris · eyelashes · lower eyelid · choroid · retina · sclera · optic nerve

MUSCLES OF EYE

superior oblique · superior rectus · lateral rectus · inferior rectus

eyebrow · eyelashes · lacrimal duct · lacrimal gland · conjunctiva · pupil · eyelids

PROTECTIVE STRUCTURES OF EYE

Seeing organs. The sense of sight is located in the eyes. Each eye consists of an eyeball and its adjacent structures. The eyeball is almost spherical — 1 inch (2.5 cm) in diameter. It has two internal cavities, or humors — the aqueous and vitreous — filled with transparent fluids. The wall of the eyeball is made up of three overlapping opaque layers of membranes: sclera, choroid, and retina.

The eyeball's outer membrane layer is the sclera. This tissue layer is hard, resistant, and white. It shapes and protects the eyeball. The anterior, or front, of the sclera is transparent, and it curves to form the cornea. The posterior, or back, of the sclera has an opening through which the optic nerve passes.

The choroid is the middle membrane. It is soft, dark in color, and contains many blood vessels that supply nutrients to the cells of the three membranes.

The iris is located in the front, or anterior, of the eyeball. This is a colored disk with a central opening called the pupil. The crystalline lens lies behind the iris. It is solid, elastic, transparent, and shaped like a biconvex lens.

The inner layer is the retina, which lines the inside of the eyeball. The retina contains two kinds of photo-sensory cells: rods and cones.

The brain makes sure both eyes move simultaneously. Six muscles are attached to each eyeball, and these turn the eyes in various directions.

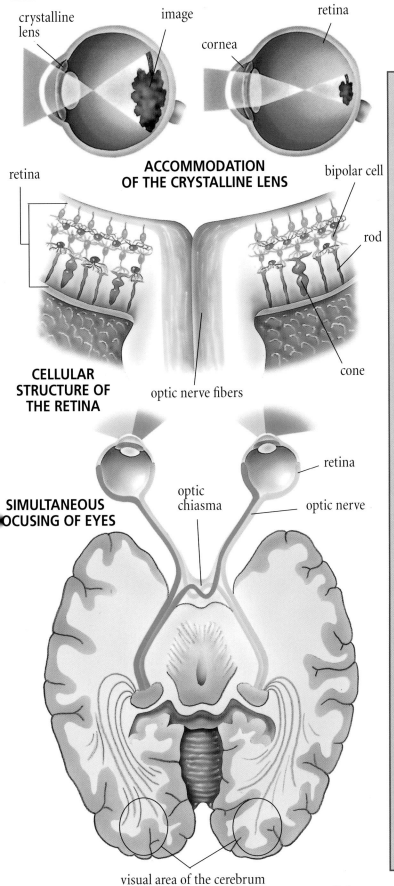

crystalline lens

image

retina

cornea

ACCOMMODATION OF THE CRYSTALLINE LENS

retina

bipolar cell

rod

cone

CELLULAR STRUCTURE OF THE RETINA

optic nerve fibers

SIMULTANEOUS FOCUSING OF EYES

retina

optic chiasma

optic nerve

visual area of the cerebrum

Eye protection. The delicate eye needs to be protected from shock, dust, smoke, bright light, and other injuries. Eyebrows keep sweat from dripping into the eyes. Eyelids shield the eye from small particles. Eyelashes screen out excess light and also catch tiny particles. Lacrimal glands produce tears, a salty water that moistens and cleans the eye; tears also contain a disinfectant that protects the eye from bacteria. The pupil controls the amount of light entering the eye; it uses muscle cells to contract the opening when there is too much light and to dilate it in dim light.

Focusing. The eye has to be able to see objects at various distances. This ability is known as accommodation. It is made possible by the crystalline lens changing its shape. In this way, images are focused automatically so that the eye can see objects clearly.

Retina. In the retina, 125 million rods and 7 million cones can be found. Rods detect changes in the intensity of light; cones see in color. Rods and cones change light rays into nerve impulses. In rods, light chemically breaks down rhodopsin, a pigment, which produces electrical impulses. In cones, the wavelength of light causes different chemical reactions that generate electrical impulses. The impulses from rods and cones travel through the optic nerve to the optic lobe of the brain.

Seeing depth. Two eyes together can see objects in three dimensions. This is called binocular vision. The pupils are about 2.5 inches (6 cm) apart, so each eye sees the same object from a different angle. The brain combines the information into a single, three-dimensional image.

The Ear

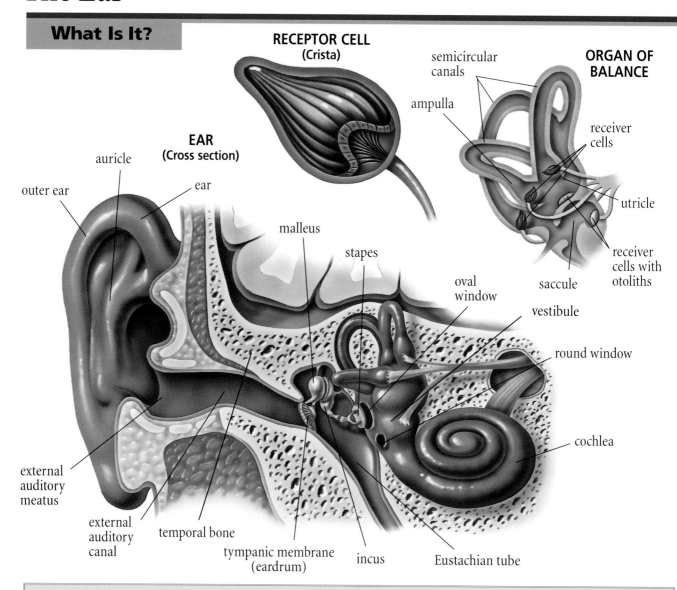

RECEPTOR CELL
(Crista)

EAR
(Cross section)

semicircular canals

ampulla

ORGAN OF BALANCE

receiver cells

utricle

outer ear

auricle

ear

malleus

stapes

oval window

vestibule

round window

receiver cells with otoliths

saccule

cochlea

external auditory meatus

external auditory canal

temporal bone

tympanic membrane (eardrum)

incus

Eustachian tube

Hearing sounds. The ear is the organ that detects sounds. There is one ear on each side of the head. The parts of the ear are: outer ear, middle ear, and inner ear. The outer ear stands out from the head and is a cartilage structure covered with skin.

From the outer ear, the auditory, or ear, canal travels into the skull for about 1 inch (2.5 cm), ending at the eardrum. The auditory canal contains hairs and glands that secrete cerumen, or earwax, to catch and remove small particles.

The middle ear lies in a cavity within the temporal bone of the skull. It connects with the pharynx through the eustachian tube. The inner side of the eardrum links with a series of tiny bones that

articulate with one another: malleus, incus, and stapes. These bones transmit vibrations received from the eardrum. The end of the stapes fits into the oval window at the beginning of the inner ear. Nearby lies what is known as the round window.

The inner ear contains the spiral cochlea. The cochlea's interior is divided into three cavities by two membranes: the vestibular and the basilar. Each cavity is filled with fluid.

The auditory nerve is formed by nerve fibers that line the basilar membrane and supply nerves to the organ of Corti. The nerve fibers carry very sensitive ciliated cells, called hair cells. These hairlike structures are the real receptors of sound.

TRANSMISSION OF SOUND WAVES

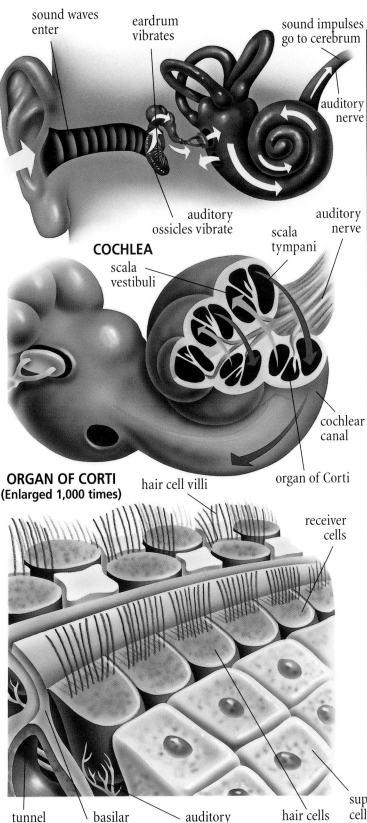

sound waves enter

eardrum vibrates

sound impulses go to cerebrum

auditory nerve

auditory ossicles vibrate

COCHLEA

scala vestibuli

scala tympani

auditory nerve

cochlear canal

organ of Corti

ORGAN OF CORTI
(Enlarged 1,000 times)

hair cell villi

receiver cells

supporting cells

tunnel of Corti

basilar membrane

auditory nerve

hair cells

Hearing sound. Sound waves are caught by the outer ear and directed down the auditory canal to vibrate the elastic eardrum. The eardrum's movements are transferred to the linked auditory ossicles. Each of these tiny bones moves the one next to it: malleus to incus to stapes. The stapes vibrates the membrane of the oval window in the cochlea. This sets up waves in the fluid inside one of the cochlear canals. The waves move the tiny hair cells of the organ of Corti, generating electrical signals that travel along the auditory nerve to the brain. There, the impulses are interpreted as sounds.

Balancing. The organ of balance is formed by the three semicircular canals and two membranous sacs: utricle and saccule. The three semicircular canals (superior, posterior, and external) are at angles to one another, so they can detect movement in any direction. They begin and end in the vestibule, a space that lies between the semicircular canals and the cochlea.

The crista. One end of each canal enlarges to form the ampulla, which houses a crista that contains hair cells. Endolymph, a fluid, fills the canals. Changes in body position set up waves in the fluid, which move the hair cells of the crista. This sends information to the brain about the position of the body when it is in motion.

The utricle and saccule in the vestibule have hair cells that are moved by gravity to tell the brain the body's position at rest.

The Sense of Taste

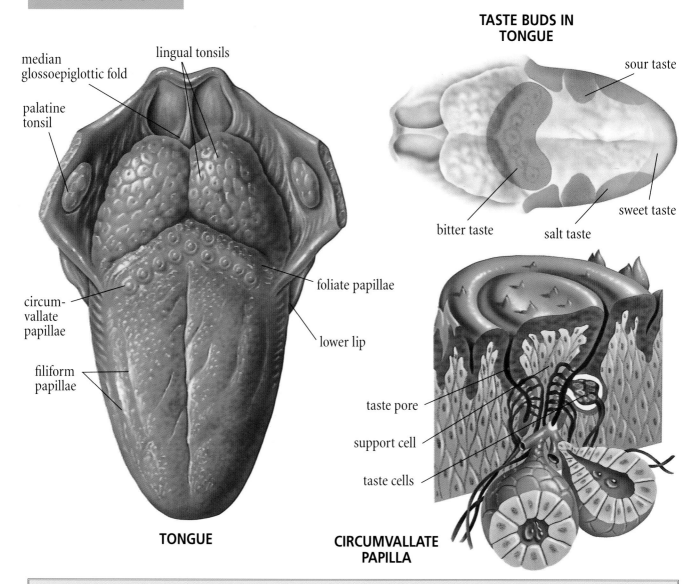

median glossoepiglottic fold

lingual tonsils

palatine tonsil

circum-vallate papillae

filiform papillae

foliate papillae

lower lip

TONGUE

TASTE BUDS IN TONGUE

sour taste

sweet taste

salt taste

bitter taste

taste pore

support cell

taste cells

CIRCUMVALLATE PAPILLA

Flavor detectors. Taste buds, or sensory cells of taste, are what are known as chemoreceptors that react to chemical stimuli. Taste buds are located on the sides of papillae at the back and sides of the tongue. There are also taste buds in the epiglottis, the soft palate, and the pharynx. Taste buds are approximately 0.0028 inch (70 microns) deep and 0.0016 inch (40 microns) across.

The kinds of papillae are: fungiform (mushroom shaped), circumvallate (shaped like a circular wall), foliate (leaflike), and filiform (threadlike). The fungiform, circumvallate, and foliate papillae have taste buds, which are the structures that detect flavors. The filiform papillae are able to detect only the sensations of heat and texture. Each taste bud has between 5 and 100 taste cells, covered with chemoreceptors. These communicate with the mouth through the taste pore. When stimulated, the taste cells generate a nervous impulse, which is transmitted by neurons.

Located in the surface of the tongue are about 10,000 taste buds. Their cells live for only about ten days, constantly being replaced by new ones. The number of taste buds diminishes with age. Children have more taste buds than adults. As a result, children are able to distinguish flavors much better.

PATH OF TASTE SENSATION TO CEREBRUM

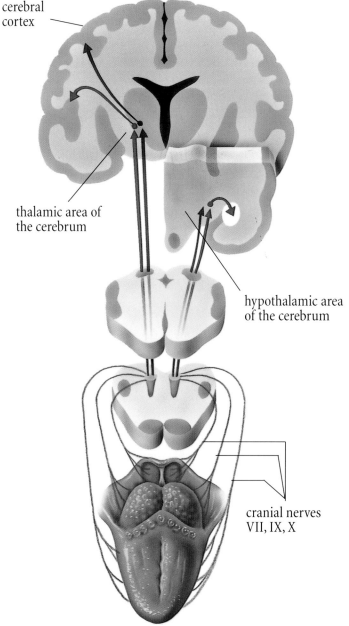

cerebral cortex

thalamic area of the cerebrum

hypothalamic area of the cerebrum

cranial nerves VII, IX, X

Sensing taste. Flavor is a very particular sensation that depends on a combination of taste, smell, and touch. Taste allows us to choose food, identifying the solid and liquid substances mixed with saliva. A substance must be in liquid form to stimulate taste cells. Saliva dissolves the solids in our mouth. There are four main sensations: sour, salty, sweet, and bitter. As a result, the flavor of each kind of food is made up from the combinations of these basic tastes. The easiest taste to detect is bitter, followed by sour, salty, and sweet.

When we eat, a bit of dissolved food penetrates the taste bud through the pore, and this stimulates the receptor neurons. It also stimulates the neuron at the base of the papilla. The stimulated neuron tells the brain about the taste in our mouth.

Taste buds are scattered in the tongue. This makes some areas more sensitive than others to certain tastes. For instance, the taste buds sensitive to sweet taste are in the front part of the tongue. Taste buds sensitive to a sour taste are concentrated on both sides of the tongue. Bitterness is best detected on the back surface of the tongue. Taste buds stimulated by a salty taste are distributed around the tongue.

PAPILLA
(Top view)

PAPILLAE

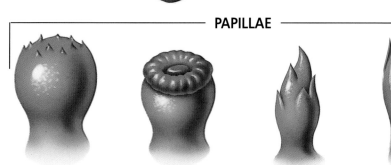

fungiform	circumvallate	foliate	filiform

(Detect flavors) — (left group)

(Detect heat and texture) — filiform

The Sense of Smell

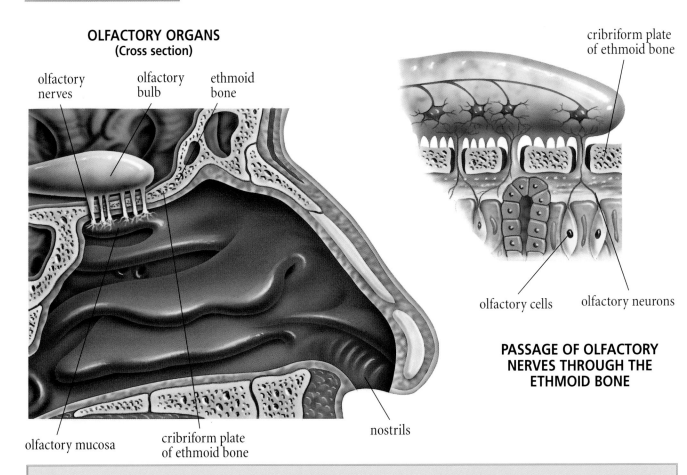

OLFACTORY ORGANS
(Cross section)

olfactory nerves

olfactory bulb

ethmoid bone

cribriform plate of ethmoid bone

olfactory cells

olfactory neurons

PASSAGE OF OLFACTORY NERVES THROUGH THE ETHMOID BONE

olfactory mucosa

cribriform plate of ethmoid bone

nostrils

Capturing odors. The sense of smell is located inside the nasal fossae, or cavities. The olfactory mucous membrane is in the upper part of the nose, and it detects gaseous substances.

The nasal fossae are two large cavities, divided by the nasal septum and lined with yellow mucous membrane in the upper part and red mucous membrane in the lower part.

The red mucous membrane is well supplied with numerous blood vessels that heat the inhaled air. The yellow membrane is the olfactory mucous membrane, possessing chemoreceptors that detect odors. It is formed from column-shaped epithelial cells and occupies 1 square inch (6.5 square cm) in the upper part of each nasal fossae.

Stimuli from the olfactory cells travel along the olfactory neurons, which pass through the openings of the cribriform plate of the ethmoid bone to the olfactory bulb of the brain. The olfactory membrane has three layers of cells and several mucous glands. Included in this are cells that secrete a mucus that keeps the olfactory epithelium clean and moist.

Columnar epithelial cells support the olfactory cells. At their free end, they form a cuticle with perforations through which nerve cell endings pass.

Olfactory cells detect the chemical stimuli of gaseous particles. There are 10 million olfactory cells in the olfactory epithelium between the support cells. The mucous ends of the olfactory cells form swellings from which five cilia, or olfactory hairs, extend 0.008 inch (0.02 cm).

These olfactory hairs penetrate the mucus that covers the inner surface of the nasal cavity. When the olfactory hairs react to different smells, they produce nerve impulses.

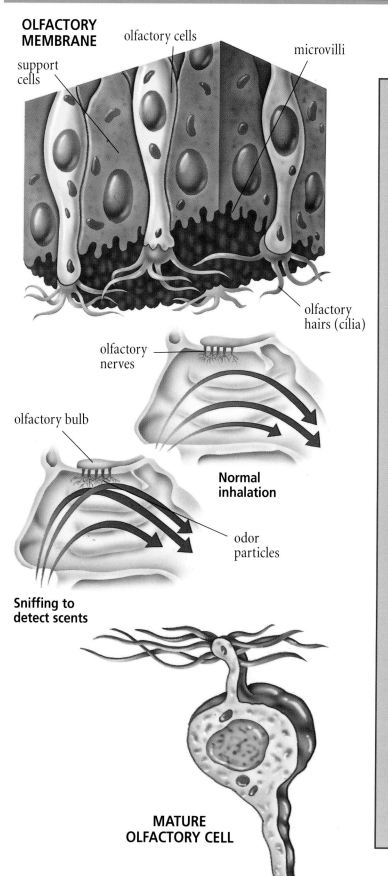

OLFACTORY MEMBRANE

support cells

olfactory cells

microvilli

olfactory hairs (cilia)

olfactory nerves

olfactory bulb

Normal inhalation

odor particles

Sniffing to detect scents

MATURE OLFACTORY CELL

Detecting scents. In order to be detected by its scent, a substance must give off vapors that can enter the nasal fossae. The substance should also be fat soluble so it can dissolve in mucus and reach the olfactory cells. Olfactory cells transmit the nerve impulse to the olfactory bulb. From there, the impulse travels to the cerebral cortex where the sensation is interpreted.

In the late 1800s, Dutch scientist Hendrik Zwaardemaker placed odors into nine classes: ethereal (i.e. fruit), aromatic (camphor), fragrant (flowers), ambrosial (musk), alliaceous (garlic), empyreumatic (smoke), caprilic (sweat), repulsive (nightshade), and nauseating (feces).

Olfactory membrane. In the lower ends of olfactory cells are olfactory knobs, from which olfactory hairs (cilia) extend. Surrounding support cells keep each olfactory cell in its place. Along each cilia lie the receptors of odor molecules, which react to the odor stimuli by generating a nervous impulse. If a person is exposed to a strong smell for too long, the sense of smell is temporarily deadened.

To detect a particular smell, people inhale more strongly than usual (sniffing) to force air to reach the olfactory grooves and bombard the cilia of the olfactory membrane with a large number of olfactory molecules.

Smell receptor cells live only a month. They detect odors for just a short time because, while maturing, they acted as support cells. New olfactory cells are constantly being produced.

The Sense of Touch

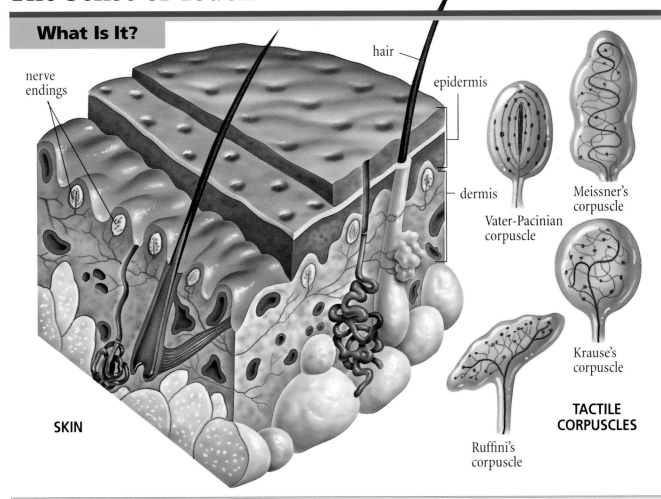

nerve endings

hair

epidermis

dermis

Vater-Pacinian corpuscle

Meissner's corpuscle

Krause's corpuscle

Ruffini's corpuscle

TACTILE CORPUSCLES

SKIN

Sensing contact. The skin measures about 18 square feet (1.7 sq. meters), weighs about 6.5 pounds (3 kg), and is the biggest organ in the body. In each square inch (sq. cm) of skin there are hundreds of nerve endings. There are about 640,000 cutaneous sensory receptors equally distributed in the body. They detect cold, heat, pressure, pain, and vibration. The receptors of touch can be free nerve endings or encapsulated nerve endings, that is, ones ending with a capsulelike shape. The encapsulated ones are known as tactile corpuscles.

The free nerve endings and the nerve endings of the hairs are sensitive to touch. For example, when an object brushes any of the hairs, these act as pivots that stimulate the adjacent sensory endings. Meissner's corpuscles are in the dermic papillae. They are 0.004 inch (100 microns) long, and they are sensitive to contact. They are particularly abundant in sensitive areas such as the fingertips — 23,220 in each square inch (6.45 sq. cm) — and tongue. These corpuscles respond and adapt very fast to the softest touch.

The Vater-Pacinian corpuscles are about 0.04 inch (1 mm) long, not very abundant, and are situated in the deepest areas of the dermis. They are sensitive to deep pressure and vibration.

The corpuscles of Krause are on the surface of the skin and detect the sensation of cold. The corpuscles of Ruffini are elongated and are located deeper in the skin than those of Krause. Ruffini's corpuscles detect the sensation of heat.

Besides being in the skin, some types of sensory receptors are also located in ligaments, muscles, tendons, and articulations (joints). These receptors send information that is used to control the rhythm of movement and muscular tension, and to determine muscle length.

THERMOREGULATION

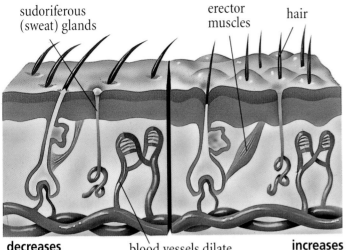

sudoriferous (sweat) glands

erector muscles

hair

decreases body heat

blood vessels dilate

increases body heat

painful sensation in cerebrum

Cooling off. The center of temperature regulation lies in the hypothalamus. It controls the production of body heat and the loss of it through the skin. When body heat increases, the hypothalamus sends instructions to the body to start sweating and to increase the flow of blood to the cutaneous vessels. Both actions help radiate heat toward the outside.

Warming up. However, when body temperature decreases, instructions are sent to contract the most superficial vessels, interrupt sweating, and contract the erector muscles of hairs. The hairs stand on end, forming an insulating layer. If temperatures are very cold, the body also starts trembling to produce heat.

Pain. Pain is an alarm that something is wrong. Some areas of the body are more sensitive to pain than others. Every time any tissue is damaged, pain is sensed. This causes the body to react to avoid further damage. Pain also reveals information about the state of the internal organs. The pain is received by nerve endings in the skin and organs. Any sensation of cold, heat, or pressure can also become painful.

urgent warning to spinal cord

stimulus

INTERPRETATION OF A STIMULUS AS PAIN

Glossary

acetylcholine — chemical neurotransmitter used to carry nerve impulses across the synaptic space between neurons or between neurons and muscle cells.

adrenaline — hormone secreted by the adrenal glands in response to sympathetic stimulation. Adrenaline increases heart rate and respiration.

afferent — carrying toward a center or main part.

anterior — toward the front; ventral.

autonomic nervous system — a system that regulates the function of organs in the body, controls involuntary actions (such as secretions and peristalsis), and consists of the sympathetic and parasympathetic nervous systems.

axon — a long, thin extension of a neuron that carries impulses away from the cell body.

biconvex — convex, or curved outward, on both sides.

central nervous system — the brain and the spinal cord.

cerebellum — a small, posterior section of the brain responsible for many subconscious skeletal muscle functions, such as coordination and muscle tone.

cerebral cortex — the gray matter on the surface of the cerebrum, including special areas, such as motor, sensory, auditory, visual, taste, olfactory, speech, and association centers.

cerebrum — the largest section of the brain. It consists of two halves, or hemispheres.

cilia — thin, movable filaments projecting from a cell membrane; sometimes called cell hairs.

cortex — the outer layer of an organ or other body structure, such as the brain.

dendrite — a thin, branching extension of a neuron that carries nerve impulses toward the cell body.

dorsal — toward the back; posterior.

efferent — carrying away from a center or main part.

epiglottis — a cartilage flap over the entrance to the larynx. It prevents food from entering the trachea during swallowing.

epithelial cells — cells of tissue found on surfaces inside and outside of the body. Epithelial cells make up skin and mucous membrane.

ganglion — a group of neuron bodies outside the brain and spinal cord.

hormone — a glandular chemical secretion produced by an organ or part of the body, and which is transported to another organ to stimulate or inhibit its activity.

lateral — at the side; away from the body.

ligament — a tough, cordlike structure of fibrous connective tissue that connects bone to bone.

medulla oblongata — the part of the brain above the spinal cord that regulates functions such as heart rate, breathing, and blood pressure.

meninges — the three membranes that cover the brain and spinal cord.

micron — a unit of length. One micron = 0.0000394 inch.

motor neuron — an efferent nerve cell that carries impulses from the central nervous system to a muscle or gland.

mucous membrane — a thin sheet of tissue that secretes mucus, a thick liquid.

myelin — a fatty substance that forms a covering, or sheath, of axons and dendrites.

neurotransmitter — a chemical that transmits impulses between neurons or between neurons and muscle cells.

papillae — elevated, pointed projections located in the tongue.

parasympathetic nervous system — the part of the autonomic nervous system that controls the body during relaxed situations.

peripheral nervous system — the part of the nervous system that consists of the cranial and spinal nerves.

pharynx — part of the alimentary canal between the cavity of the mouth and the esophagus that forms a passage for air and food.

plexus — a network of nerves or veins.

posterior — toward the back.

rhodopsin — pigment in the rods of the eye's retina that changes light into chemical energy.

semicircular canals — three bony loops in the inner ear where receptors detect motion.

sensory neuron — an afferent nerve cell that carries impulses from a sensor to the central nervous system.

somatic — referring to body wall structures, such as skeletal muscles and skin.

spinal cord — a thick cord of nerve tissue that starts at the brain and travels down through the backbone.

stimulus — something that causes activity in a living organism; an agent that affects a sensory receptor.

sympathetic nervous system — the part of the autonomic nervous system that controls the body during stressful situations.

synapse — the space between the axon of one neuron and the cell body or dendrite of the adjacent neuron, or between the end of a motor neuron and a muscle or gland cell; also called synaptic cleft.

tendon — a tough, cordlike structure of fibrous connective tissue that connects muscle to bone.

ventral — toward the front; anterior.

vertebra — one of the many small bones that form the spine.

viscera — the organs within the body cavity.

More Books to Read

The Body. Young Scientist Concepts and Projects (series). Steve Parker (Gareth Stevens)

Brain and Nervous System. Mark Lambert (Silver Burdett)

How Our Senses Work. Jamie Ripoll (Chelsea House)

The Immune System. Edward Edelson (Chelsea House)

A Kid's Guide to the Brain. Silvia Funston and Jay Ingram (Firefly Books)

My Brain and Senses. Paul Bennett (Silver Burdett)

The Nerve Cell. Diane Ralston & Henry Ralston (Carolina Biological)

The Nervous System. Edward Edelson (Chelsea House)

The Nervous System. Alvin Silverstein, et al. (TFC Books)

The Nervous System and the Brain. (Chelsea House)

Our Bodies. Under the Microscope (series). Casey Horton (Gareth Stevens)

Videos to Watch

The Autonomic Nervous System. (International Film Bureau)

The Brain. (CLEARVU/eav, Inc.)

Human Body Systems (series). (Barr Films)

I Am Joe's Ear. (Pyramid Media)

I Am Joe's Eye. (Pyramid Media)

I Am Joe's Skin. (Pyramid Media)

Mind Your Own Body: What's a Body? (PBS)

Web Sites to Visit

www.eyenet.org/public/anatomy/anatomy.html   www.hhmi.org/senses

www.innerbody.com/htm/body.html   kidshealth.org/kid/

Some web sites stay current longer than others. For further web sites, use your browsers to locate the following topics: *anatomy, biology, brain, ears, eyes, human body, nervous system, physiology, senses,* and *skin.*

Index